MASTER

AGENDA 2.0___

M	T	W	T	F	S	S	M	T	W	T	F	S	S	M	T	W	T	F	S	S

M	T	W	T	F	S	S	M	T	W	T	F	S	S	M	T	W	T	F	S	S

M	T	W	T	F	S	S	M	T	W	T	F	S	S	M	T	W	T	F	S	S

M	T	W	T	F	S	S	M	T	W	T	F	S	S	M	T	W	T	F	S	S

INDEX

- [ ] INSPIRATIONAL BOARD

- [ ] TIPS, TRICKS & IDEAS

- [ ] DIRECTORY

- [ ] FUTURE LOG

- [ ] MONTHLY LOG

- [ ] MENU BOARD OF THE MONTH

- [ ] DAYLY LOG

COLOR CODES

● **FREE TIME AND HOBBIES**
(vacation, watch TV, surf the internet, listen to Radio, read, gaming)

● **HOME AND GARDEN** (clean up, wash, ironing, do dishes, reparations, general gardening)

● **SOCIALITÉ** (share with family/friends/partner, birthday, party, meeting, events)

● **FESTIVITY AND CULTURE**
(shows, theatre, museum, cultural events, stand ups)

● **HEALTH AND BEAUTY** (hair, exercise, doctor, diet, treatments, personal development)

● **FINANCES** (business, company, various incomes, foundation, donations)

● **MY CREATIONS** (musical instruments, drawing, writing, blogging, crafting)

DIRECTORY

MORNING Notes:

Evening Notes:

Night Notes:

Inspirational Board

Stick something

Write something

What's funny?

Draw something

Sing something

Tips, Tricks

& Ideas

Future log

Birthdays, Holidays, special events, future activities, long term plan.

M	T	W	T	F	S	S

M	T	W	T	F	S	S

M	T	W	T	F	S	S

M	T	W	T	F	S	S

NOTES: Fact, Idea, Thought, Observation

Monthly log

_____

1 -
2 -
3 -
4 -
5 -
6 -
7 -
8 -
9 -
10 -
11 -
12 -
13 -
14 -
15 -
16 -
17 -
18 -
19 -
20 -
21 -
22 -
23 -
24 -
25 -
26 -
27 -
28 -
29 -
30 -
31 -

TASKS OF THE MONTH

Menu Board

WEEKS	BREAKFAST	LUNCH	SNAK
1			
2			
3			
4			
5			

Of The Month

DINNER	SHOPPING LIST

Daily log:

*"You yourself,
as much as anybody in the entire universe,
deserve your love and affection."
- Buddha*

*"Until you value yourself,
you won't value your time.
Until you value your time,
you will not do anything with it."
– M. Scott Peck*

*"A man cannot be comfortable
without his own approval."
– Mark Twain*

*"Never be bullied into silence.
Never allow yourself to be made a victim.
Accept no one's definition of your life,
but define yourself."
- Harvey Fierstein*

*"Love yourself first
and everything else falls into line.
You really have to love yourself
to get anything done in this world."
- Lucille Ball*

*"Remember always
that you not only have the right
to be an individual,
you have an obligation to be one."
- Eleanor Roosevelt*

"If only you could sense
how important you are
to the lives of those you meet;
how important you can be
to people you may never even dream of.
There is something of yourself
that you leave at every meeting
with another person."
— Fred Rogers

"Low self-esteem is like driving through life with your hand-break on."
― Maxwell Maltz

*"What lies behind us
and what lies before us
are tiny matters
compared to what lies within us."
– Ralph Waldo Emerson*

*"When you recover or discover something
that nourishes your soul and brings joy,
care enough about yourself
to make room for it in your life."
– Jean Shinoda Bolen*

*"Self-care is never a selfish act
—it is simply good stewardship
of the only gift I have,
the gift I was put on earth to offer to others."
– Parker Palmer*

"Why should we worry about what others think of us, do we have more confidence in their opinions than we do our own?"
- Brigham Young

*"To fall in love with yourself
is the first secret to happiness."
– Robert Morley*

*"Don't waste your energy
trying to change opinions ...
Do your thing, and don't care if they like it."
- Tina Fey*

"So then, the relationship of self to other
is the complete realization
that loving yourself is impossible
without loving everything defined
as other than yourself."
– Alan Watts

*"Owning our story and loving ourselves
through that process
is the bravest thing that we'll ever do."
- Brené Brown*

*"One of the greatest regrets in life
is being what others would want you to be,
rather than being yourself."
– Shannon L. Alder*

*Inaction breeds doubt and fear.
Action breeds confidence and courage.
If you want to conquer fear,
do not sit home and think about it.
Go out and get busy."
– Dale Carnegie*

*"Once you embrace your value,
talents and strengths,
it neutralizes when others think less of you."
- Rob Liano*

*"To accept ourselves
as we are means to value our imperfections
as much as our perfections."
- Sandra Bierig*

*"To establish true self-esteem
we must concentrate on our successes
and forget about the failures
and the negatives in our lives."
– Denis Waitley*

*"Our self-respect tracks our choices.
Every time we act in harmony
with our authentic self and our heart,
we earn our respect.
It is that simple. Every choice matters."
– Dan Coppersmith*

"Don't rely on someone else
for your happiness and self-worth.
Only you can be responsible for that.
If you can't love and respect yourself
no one else will be able to make that happen.
Accept who you are – completely;
the good and the bad –
and make changes as YOU see fit –
not because you think
someone else wants you to be different."
– Stacey Charter

*"Don't ask yourself what the world needs,
ask yourself what makes you come alive.
And then go and do that.
Because what the world needs
is people who have come alive."
– Howard Washington Thurman*

*"If you don't love yourself,
nobody will. Not only that,
you won't be good at loving anyone else.
Loving starts with the self."
- Wayne Dyer*

*"The worst loneliness
is to not be comfortable with yourself."
– Mark Twain*

*"My best friend is the one
who brings out the best in me."
– Henry Ford*

*"No other love no matter how genuine it is,
can fulfill one's heart
better than unconditional self-love."
– Edmond Mbiaka*

"Loving yourself isn't vanity. It's sanity."
– Katrina Mayer

*"Lighten up on yourself.
No one is perfect.
Gently accept your humanness."
– Deborah Day*

*"Too many people overvalue what they are not
and undervalue what they are."*
- Malcolm S. Forbes

*"Never bend your head.
Always hold it high.
Look the world straight in the face."
- Helen Keller*

*"You have been criticizing yourself for years, and it hasn't worked.
Try approving of yourself and see what happens."*
— Louise L. Hay

*"To love oneself
is the beginning of a life-long romance"
– Oscar Wilde*

"Be faithful to that which exists within yourself."
– André Gide

"Act as if what you do makes a difference. It does."
- William James

"The most beautiful people we have known
are those who have known defeat,
known suffering, known struggle,
known loss, and have found their way out of the depths.
These persons have an appreciation,
a sensitivity and an understanding of life
that fills them with compassions, gentleness,
and a deep loving concern.
Beautiful people do not just happen."
– Elizabeth Kubler-Ross

*"You have to believe in yourself
when no one else does
that makes you a winner right here."
– Venus Williams*

*"If you do not respect your own wishes,
no one else will.
You will simply attract people
who disrespect you as much as you do."
- Vironika Tugaleva*

*"I had to grow to love my body.
I did not have a good self-image at first.
Finally it occurred to me,
I'm either going to love me or hate me.
And I chose to love myself.
Then everything kind of sprung from there.
Things that I thought weren't attractive
became sexy. Confidence makes you sexy."
– Queen Latifah*

*"If you have the ability to love,
love yourself first."
- Charles Bukowski*

*"To be yourself in a world
that is constantly trying
to make you something else
is the greatest accomplishment."
– Ralph Waldo Emerson*

*"People who love themselves,
don't hurt other people.
The more we hate ourselves,
the more we want others to suffer."
- Dan Pearce*

*"Love is the great miracle cure.
Loving ourselves works miracles in our lives."
- Louise Hay*

*"The real difficulty is to overcome
how you think about yourself."*
- Maya Angelou

*"Love yourself enough to set boundaries.
Your time and energy are precious.
You get to choose how you use it.
You teach people how to treat you
by deciding what you will and won't accept."
– Anna Taylor*

*"The most terrifying thing
is to accept oneself completely."
- Carl Gustav Jung*

*"You're always with yourself,
so you might as well enjoy the company."
- Diane Von Furstenberg*

"Beauty begins the moment you decided to be yourself."
- Coco Chanel

*"If you aren't good at loving yourself,
you will have a difficult time loving anyone,
since you'll resent the time and energy
you give another person
that you aren't even giving to yourself."
- Barbara De Angelis*

"It's surprising how many persons
go through life without ever recognizing
that their feelings toward other people
are largely determined
by their feelings toward themselves,
and if you're not comfortable within yourself,
you can't be comfortable with others."
- Sidney J. Harris

*"When I loved myself enough,
I began leaving whatever wasn't healthy.
This meant people, jobs, my own beliefs and habits
anything that kept me small.
My judgement called it disloyal.
Now I see it as self-loving."
- Kim McMillen*

*"Don't rely on someone else
for your happiness and self-worth.
Only you can be responsible for that.
If you can't love and respect yourself
no one else will be able to make that happen.
Accept who you are – completely;
the good and the bad –
and make changes as YOU see fit –
not because you think
someone else wants you to be different."
– Stacey Charter*

"Don't ask yourself what the world needs,
ask yourself what makes you come alive.
And then go and do that.
Because what the world needs
is people who have come alive."
- Howard Washington Thurman

> "If you don't love yourself,
> nobody will. Not only that,
> you won't be good at loving anyone else.
> Loving starts with the self."
> – Wayne Dyer

*"The worst loneliness
is to not be comfortable with yourself."
- Mark Twain*

*"My best friend is the one
who brings out the best in me."
- Henry Ford*

*"No other love no matter how genuine it is,
can fulfill one's heart
better than unconditional self-love."
– Edmond Mbiaka*

"Loving yourself isn't vanity. It's sanity."
– Katrina Mayer

*"Lighten up on yourself.
No one is perfect.
Gently accept your humanness."
– Deborah Day*

*"Too many people overvalue what they are not
and undervalue what they are."*
– Malcolm S. Forbes

*"Never bend your head.
Always hold it high.
Look the world straight in the face."*
- Helen Keller

*"You have been criticizing yourself for years,
and it hasn't worked.
Try approving of yourself
and see what happens."
- Louise L. Hay*

*"To love oneself
is the beginning of a life-long romance"
– Oscar Wilde*

"Be faithful to that which exists within yourself."
– André Gide

"Act as if what you do makes a difference. It does."
– William James

"The most beautiful people we have known
are those who have known defeat,
known suffering, known struggle,
known loss, and have found their way out of the depths.
These persons have an appreciation,
a sensitivity and an understanding of life
that fills them with compassions, gentleness,
and a deep loving concern.
Beautiful people do not just happen."
– Elizabeth Kubler-Ross

*"You have to believe in yourself
when no one else does
that makes you a winner right here."
– Venus Williams*

*"If you do not respect your own wishes,
no one else will.
You will simply attract people
who disrespect you as much as you do."
– Vironika Tugaleva*

"I had to grow to love my body.
I did not have a good self-image at first.
Finally it occurred to me,
I'm either going to love me or hate me.
And I chose to love myself.
Then everything kind of sprung from there.
Things that I thought weren't attractive
became sexy. Confidence makes you sexy."
– Queen Latifah

*"If you have the ability to love,
love yourself first."*
- Charles Bukowski

"To be yourself in a world
that is constantly trying
to make you something else
is the greatest accomplishment."
- Ralph Waldo Emerson

*"People who love themselves,
don't hurt other people.
The more we hate ourselves,
the more we want others to suffer."
- Dan Pearce*

*"Love is the great miracle cure.
Loving ourselves works miracles in our lives."
– Louise Hay*

*"The real difficulty is to overcome
how you think about yourself."
– Maya Angelou*

*"Love yourself enough to set boundaries.
Your time and energy are precious.
You get to choose how you use it.
You teach people how to treat you
by deciding what you will and won't accept."
- Anna Taylor*

*"The most terrifying thing
is to accept oneself completely."
– Carl Gustav Jung*

"You're always with yourself,
so you might as well enjoy the company."
– Diane Von Furstenberg

"Beauty begins the moment you decided to be yourself."
– Coco Chanel

*"If you aren't good at loving yourself,
you will have a difficult time loving anyone,
since you'll resent the time and energy
you give another person
that you aren't even giving to yourself."
— Barbara De Angelis*

"Be faithful to that which exists within yourself."
— André Gide

"Be faithful to that which exists within yourself."
– André Gide